AARON COPLAND

Old American Songs
Complete

HIRSCHFELD 60

BOOSEY & HAWKES

AN IMAGEM COMPANY

DISTRIBUTED BY
HAL•LEONARD®
CORPORATION
7777 W. BLUEMOUND RD. P.O. BOX 13819 MILWAUKEE, WI 53213

www.boosey.com
www.halleonard.com

The first set of *Old American Songs* was completed in 1950, the same year that Copland finished his other major song set, *Twelve Poems of Emily Dickinson.* While Copland was writing the songs, tenor Peter Pears and composer Benjamin Britten came to visit him. Taken by Copland's new settings, they left with his promise of receiving copies of the songs in England to perform. On October 17, 1950, the first set was given its world premiere by Pears with Britten at the piano at their Aldeburgh Festival. The American premiere took place in New York on January 28, 1951, with Copland accompanying baritone William Warfield. The success of the first set prompted Copland to set five more songs. Finished in 1952, the second set was premiered by Warfield and Copland at the Castle Hill Concerts in Massachusetts on July 24 of that year. Copland would later orchestrate both sets for medium voice and small orchestra. Warfield sang the premiere of the orchestrated first set with the Los Angeles Philharmonic, conducted by Alfred Wallenstein, on January 7, 1955. Grace Bumbry premiered the second set with the Ojai Festival Orchestra on May 25, 1955, with Copland on the podium.

Contents

FIRST SET

1. *The Boatmen's Dance*
   Published in Boston in 1843 as an "original banjo melody" by Old Dan. D. Emmett, who later composed *Dixie*. From the Harris Collection of American Poetry and Plays in Brown University.

2. *The Dodger*
   As sung by Mrs. Emma Dusenberry of Mena, Arkansas, who learned it in the 1880's. Supposedly used in the Cleveland-Blaine presidential campaign. Published by John A. and Alan Lomax in *Our Singing Country*.

3. *Long Time Ago*
   Issued in 1837 by George Pope Morris, who adapted the words, and Charles Edward Horn, who arranged the music from an anonymous, original minstrel tune. Also from the Harris Collection.

4. *Simple Gifts*
   A favorite song of the Shaker sect, from the period 1837-1847. The melody and words were quoted by Edward D. Andrews in his book of Shaker rituals, songs and dances, entitled *The Gift To Be Simple*.

5. *I Bought Me a Cat*
   A children's nonsense song. This version was sung to the composer by the American playwright Lynn Riggs, who learned it during his boyhood in Oklahoma.

SECOND SET

1. *The Little Horses*
   A children's lullaby song originating in the Southern States – date unknown. This adaptation founded in part on John A. and Alan Lomax's version in *Folk Song U.S.A.*

2. *Zion's Walls*
   A revivalist song. Original melody and words credited to John G. McCurry, compiler of the *Social Harp*. Published by George P. Jackson in *Down East Spirituals*.

3. *The Golden Willow Tree*
   Variant of the well-known Anglo-American ballad, more usually called *The Golden Vanity*. This version is based on a recording issued by the Library of Congress Music Division from its collection of the Archive of American Folk Song. Justus Begley recorded it with banjo accompaniment for Alan and Elizabeth Lomax in 1937.

4. *At the River*
   Hymn Tune. Words and melody are by Rev. Robert Lowry, 1865.

5. *Ching-a-ring Chaw*
   Minstrel Song. The words have been adapted from the original, in the Harris Collection of American Poetry and Plays in Brown University.

Old American Songs

FIRST SET

1. THE BOATMEN'S DANCE

(Minstrel Song-1843)

original key: E Major

Arranged by
AARON COPLAND

2nd time

As at first (♪ = 63)

High row the boat-men row float-in' down the riv - er the O - hi - o. ___

Fast tempo (♩ = 126)

3.The boat - man is a thrift - y man There's none can do as the

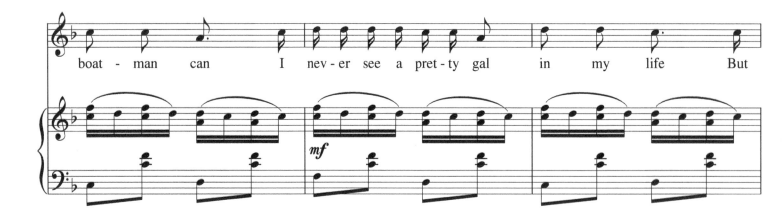

boat - man can I nev - er see a pret -ty gal in my life But

that she was a boat - man's wife O dance the boat-men dance, O

(mark the bass)

dance the boat - men dance O dance all night 'til broad day - light and go

As at first (♪ = 63)

home with the gals in the morn - in'. High row the boat - men row

float - in' down the riv - er, the O - hi - o, High row the

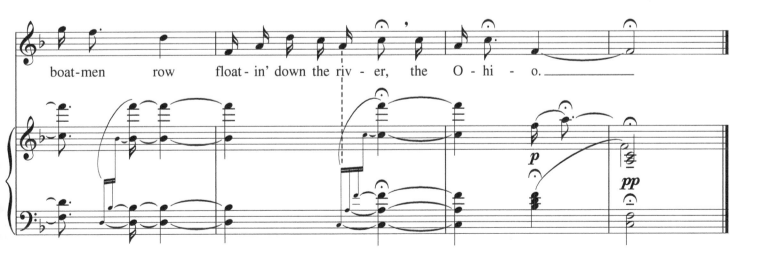

boat-men row float - in' down the riv - er, the O - hi - o.

2. THE DODGER
(Campaign Song)
original key: G Major

Arranged by
AARON COPLAND

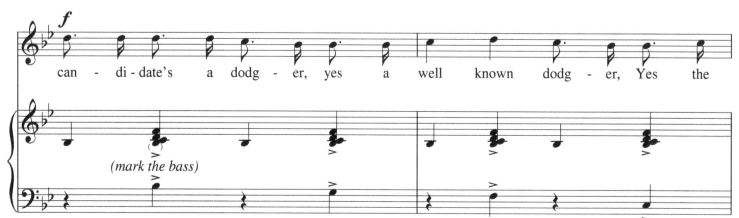

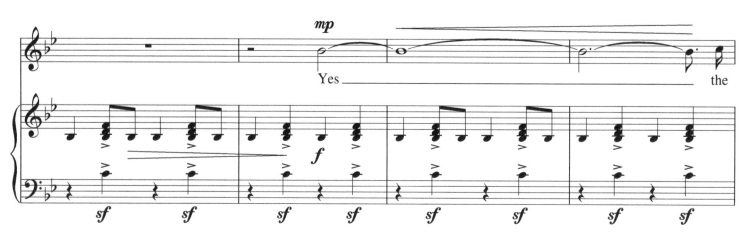

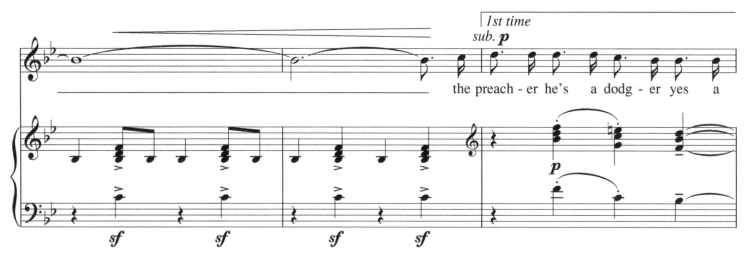

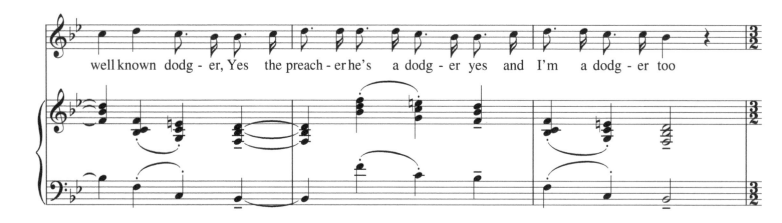

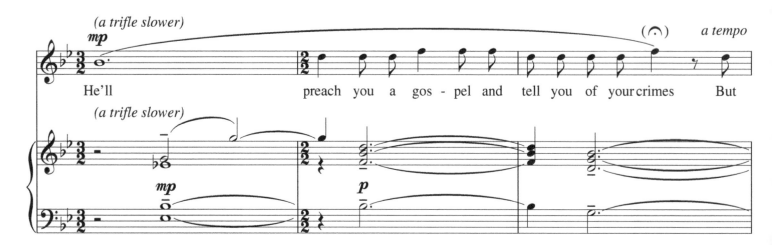

look out boys _ he's a-dodg-in' for your dimes, Yes we're all

2nd time
sub. **p**

lov - er he's a dodg - er, yes a well known dodg - er Yes the

lov - er he's a dodg - er, yes and I'm a dodg - er too

He'll hug you and kiss you and call you his bride But

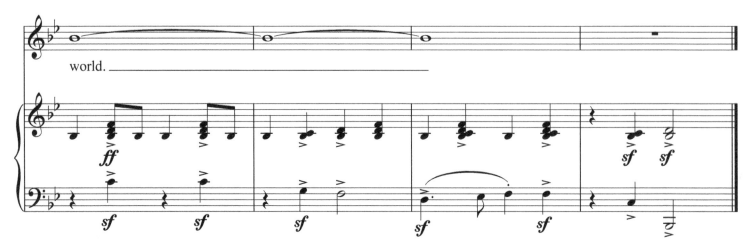

3. LONG TIME AGO
(Ballad)

original key: B♭ Major

Arranged by
AARON COPLAND

On the lake where droop'd the wil-low Long time a - go

Where the rock threw back the bil-low Bright - er ___ than snow. ___

16

Dwelt a maid be-loved and cher-ish'd By high and

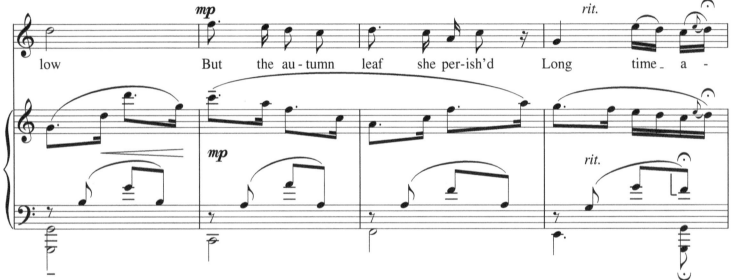

low But the au-tumn leaf she per-ish'd Long time a-

go.

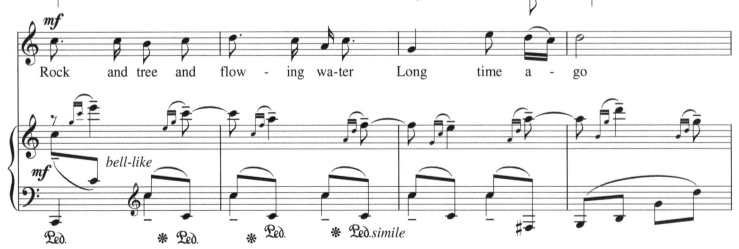

Rock and tree and flow-ing wa-ter Long time a-go

4. SIMPLE GIFTS

(Shaker Song)

original key: A♭ Major

Arranged by
AARON COPLAND

[2nd time to Coda]

love and de-light. ___ When true sim-pli-ci-ty is gained To

bow and to bend we shan't be a-shamed To turn, turn will be our de-light 'Till by

turn-ing, turn-ing we come round right. _____ 'Tis the

CODA

(dreamily)

5. I BOUGHT ME A CAT

(Children's Song)

original key: F Major

Arranged by
AARON COPLAND

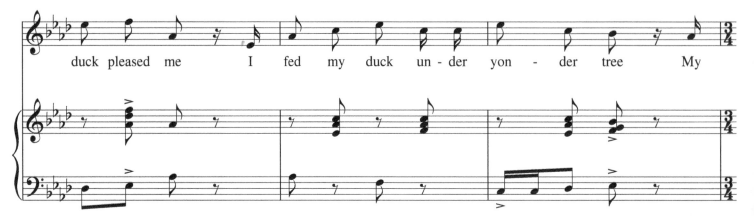

hen pleased me I fed my hen un - der yon - der tree My

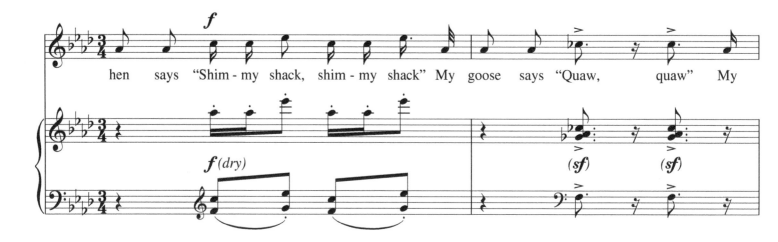

hen says "Shim - my shack, shim - my shack" My goose says "Quaw, quaw" My

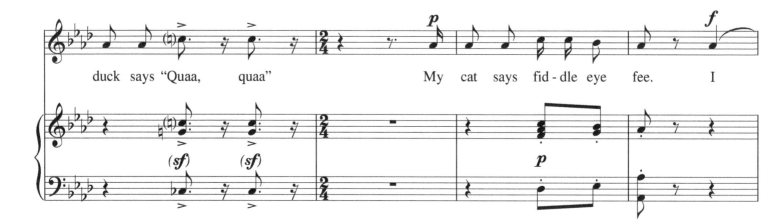

duck says "Quaa, quaa" My cat says fid - dle eye fee. I

bought me a pig My pig pleased me I fed my pig un - der yon - der tree My

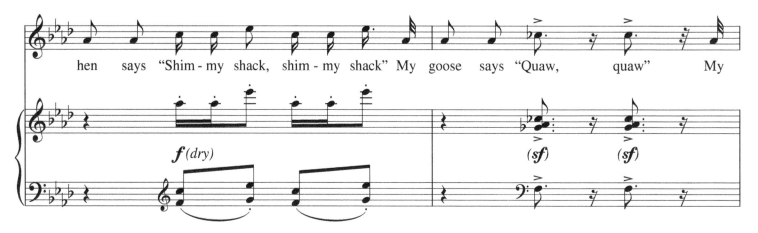

hen says "Shim - my shack, shim - my shack" My goose says "Quaw, quaw" My

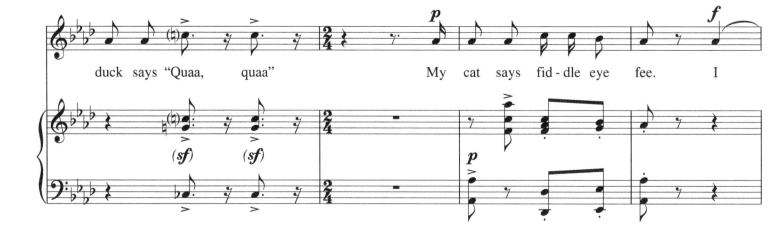

duck says "Quaa, quaa" My cat says fid - dle eye fee. I

bought me a horse My horse pleased me I fed my horse un - der

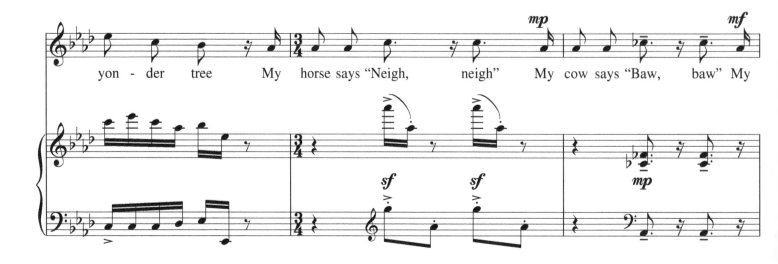

yon - der tree My horse says "Neigh, neigh" My cow says "Baw, baw" My

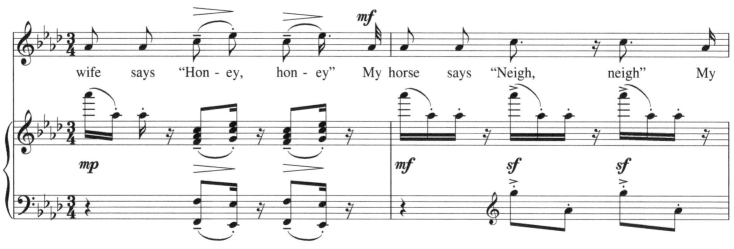

wife says "Hon - ey, hon - ey" My horse says "Neigh, neigh" My

cow says "Baw, baw" My pig says "Grif - fey, grif - fey" My

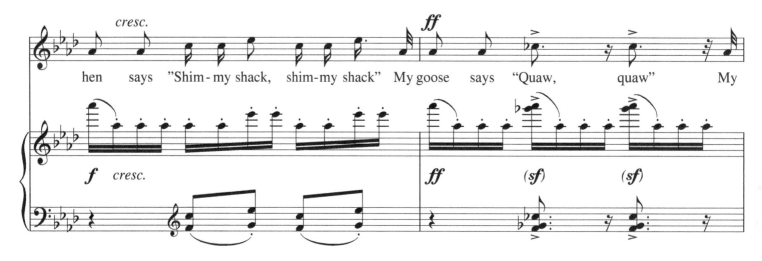

hen says "Shim - my shack, shim-my shack" My goose says "Quaw, quaw" My

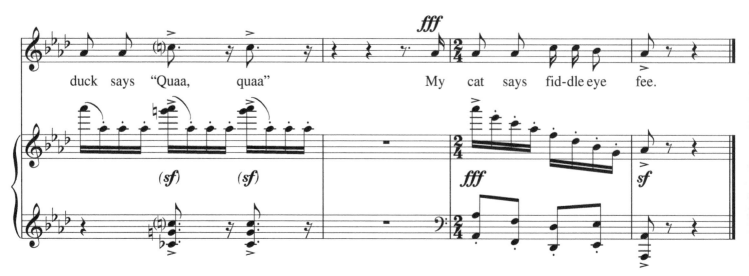

duck says "Quaa, quaa" My cat says fid-dle eye fee.

Old American Songs

SECOND SET

HIRSCHFELD 60

1. THE LITTLE HORSES

(Lullaby)

original key: E minor

Arranged by
AARON COPLAND

f
black and a bay and a brown and a gray and a Coach
(no ritard.)
più f
(long)
ad lib.
and six-a lit-tle hor-ses.
As at first (slowly)
p
Hush you bye,
a tempo
f
mf
p
Don't you cry, Oh you pret-ty lit-tle ba-by.
mp
Go to sleep-y lit-tle
mp
ba-by.
p
poco
ad lib.
Oh you pret-ty lit-tle ba-by.
p
mp

2. ZION'S WALLS

(Revivalist Song)

original key: F Major

Arranged by
AARON COPLAND

With a moderate swing (♩. = 80)

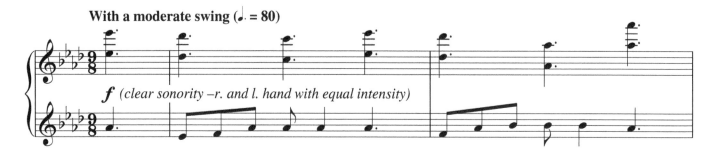

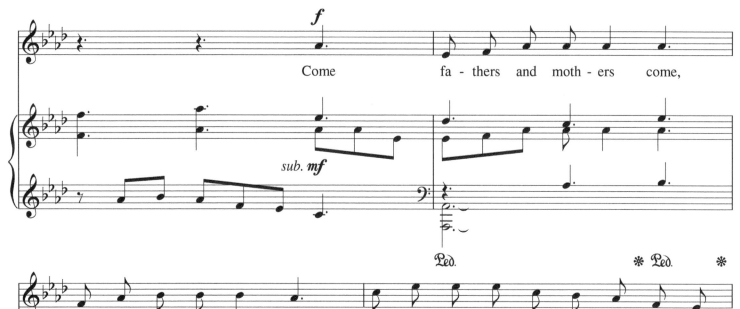

Come fa - thers and moth - ers come,

Sis - ters and broth - ers come, Join us in sing - ing the prais - es of

walls of Zi - on.

senza Ped.

_(f)_

_f_

Come fa - thers and moth - ers, Come

upper voice legato

_mf_

sis - ters and broth - ers, Come join us in

sing - ing the prais - es of Zi - on.

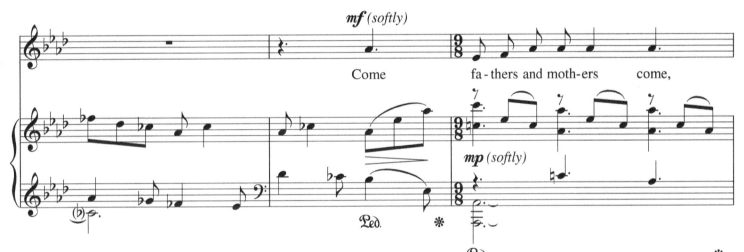

3. THE GOLDEN WILLOW TREE

(Anglo-American Ballad)

original key: G Major

Arranged by
AARON COPLAND

With gusto (♩ = 138-144)

(bright sonority, r.h. notes somewhat punched-out)

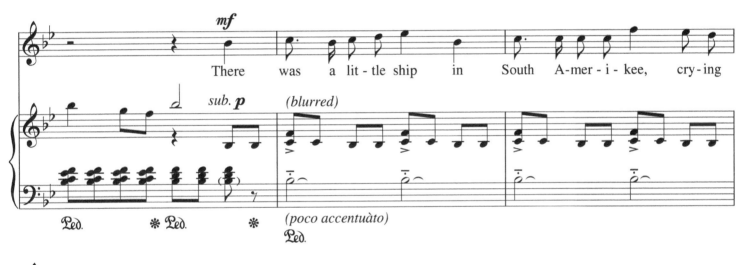

There was a lit-tle ship in South A-mer-i-kee, cry-ing

O the land that lies so low, There was a lit-tle ship in

South A-mer-i-kee, She went by the name of the

Gold-en Wil-low Tree, As she sailed in the low - land lone - some low,

As she sailed in the low - land so low. _____ We had-n't been a-sail-in' more than two weeks or three, Till we

(legato)

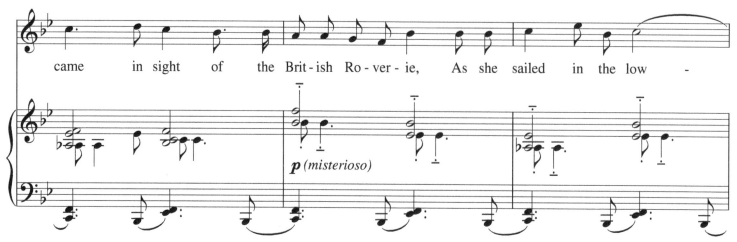

came in sight of the Brit-ish Ro-ver-ie, As she sailed in the low -

-land lone - some low, As she sailed in the low - land so

low. Up stepped a lit - tle

mf (frank and open)

mp

(half stacc.)

car-pen - ter boy Says "What will you give me for the ship that I'll des - troy?"

"I'll give you gold or I'll give thee, I'll give you gold or

f

(clouded)

mf

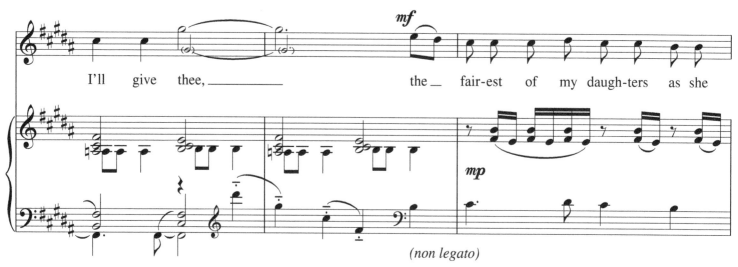

I'll give thee, _____ the _ fair-est of my daugh-ters as she

(non legato)

sails up - on the sea, If you'll sink 'em in the low -

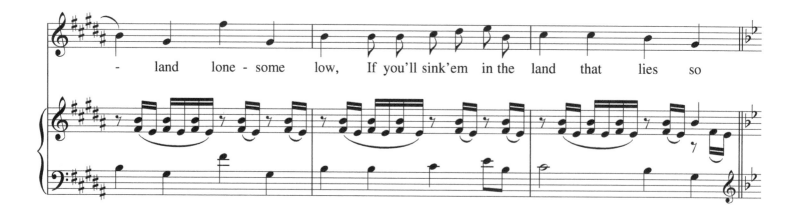

- land lone - some low, If you'll sink 'em in the land that lies so

low." _____ He

low, Though you sank 'em in the land that lies so

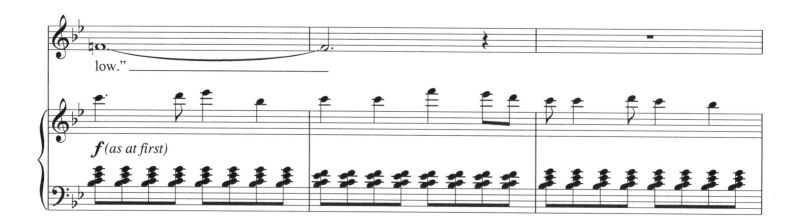

low." _____

f (as at first)

"If it was-n't for the love that I have for your men, I'd

(*p*)

do un-to you as I done un-to them, I'd sink you in the low -

8va

(*mp*)

(*poco accentuàto*)

bot - tom of the sea. _____ Sank him-

self ___ in the low - land lone - some low, Sank him - self ___ in the

land that lies so low. _____

(molto cresc.)

4. AT THE RIVER

(Hymn Tune)

original key: E♭ Major

Arranged by
AARON COPLAND

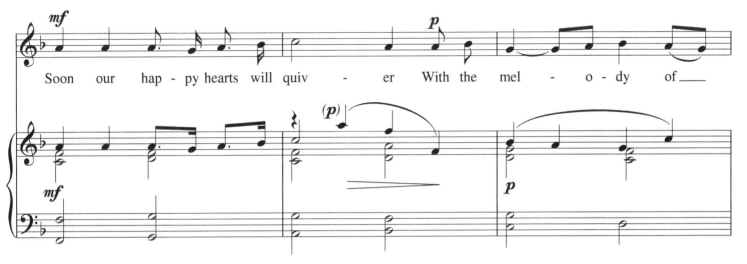

Soon our hap-py hearts will quiv - er With the mel - o - dy of __

peace. Yes we'll gath-er by the riv - er, The

beau - ti - ful, the beau - ti - ful __ riv - er, Gath - er with the saints __ by the

riv - er That flows by the throne of __ God, _____ That flows by the throne of __ God.

5. CHING-A-RING CHAW
(Minstrel Song)
original key: D Major

Arranged by
AARON COPLAND

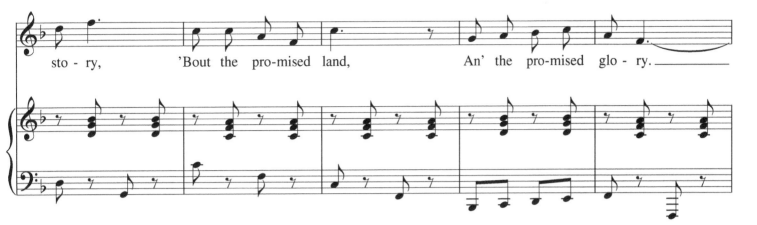

sto - ry, 'Bout the pro-mised land, An' the pro-mised glo - ry._____

_____ You don' need to fear, If you have no

(banjo style)

mon - ey, You don' need none there, to buy you milk and hon - ey._____

_____ There you'll ride in